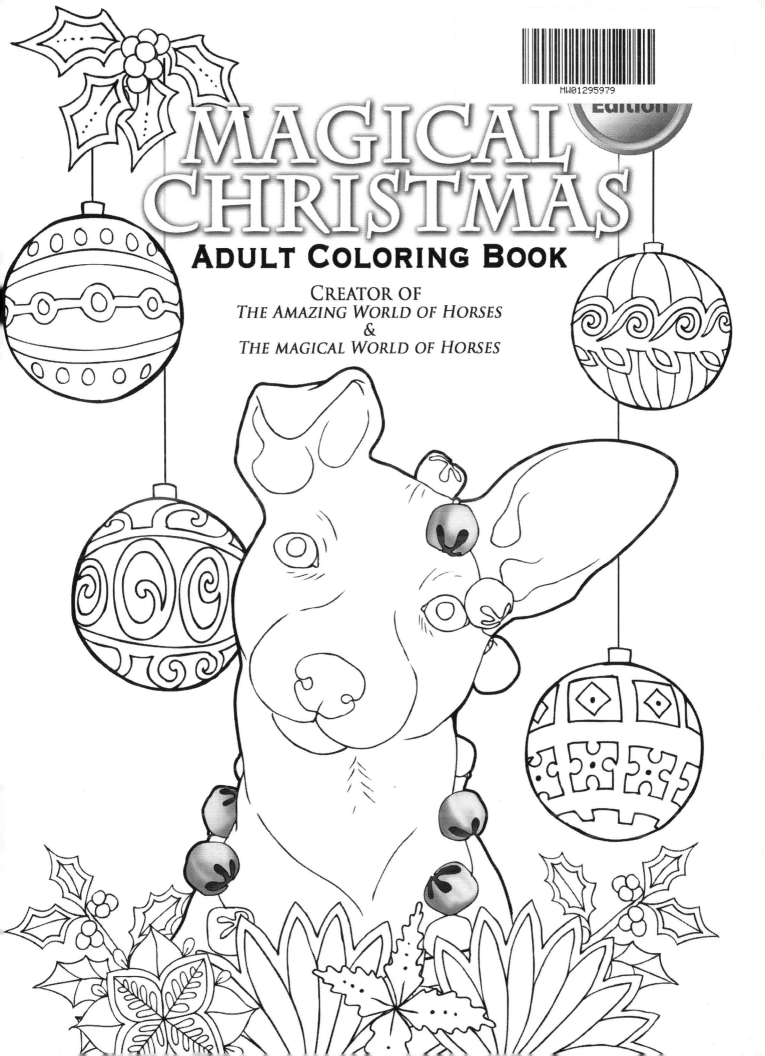

FREE COLORING PAGES EVERY MONTH!!!

Go Here To Get Free Coloring Pages Sent To Your Inbox MONTHLY!

www.freemonthlycoloringpages.pagedemo.co

All rights reserved. No part of this book may be reproduced in any form without written permission of the copyright owners. If you would like to see more images and stay updated on new coloring books, visit our web page at www.selahworks.com.
Printed in the U.S.A.

Copyright © 2016 Cindy Elsharouni
ISBN-13: 978-1539785309
ISBN-10: 1539785300

LOVE HORSES? GET THE FIRST VOLUME THE AMAZING WORLD OF HORSES

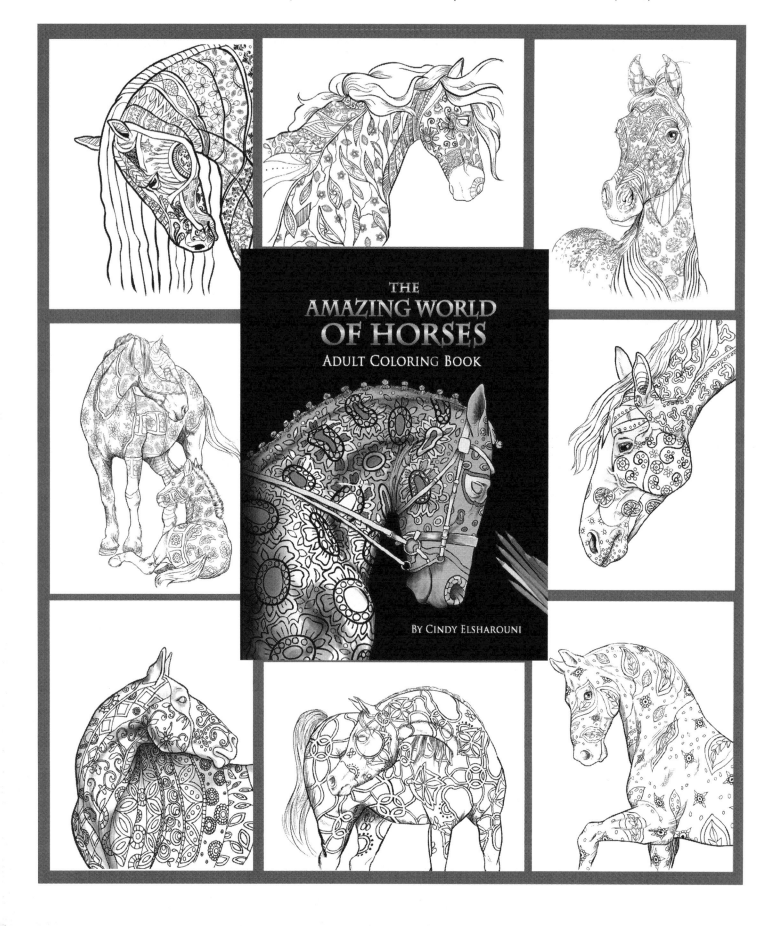

This Book Belongs To
_____

Coloring Expands Your Conciousness And Can Take You To Universes

— Cindy Elsharouni

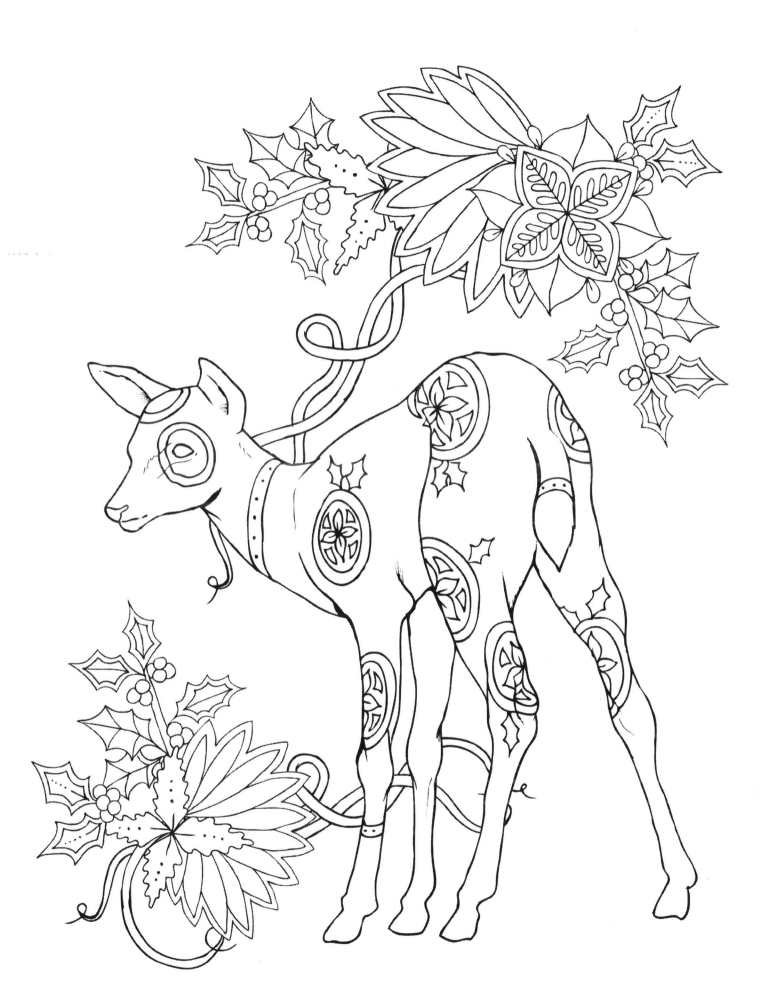

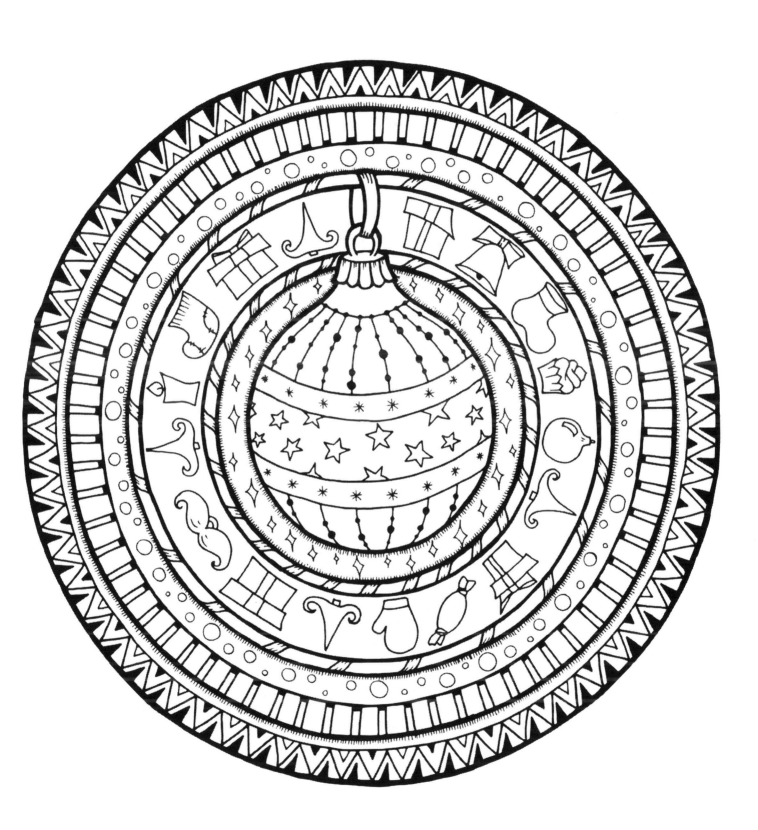

More Books By Cindy Elsharouni!
If you love horses, Dogs or just want a collection of animals, don't miss out on these books.

Available on amazon.com or www.selahworks.com

About the Artists

Cindy Elsharouni has been drawing since the age of three. She has developed into a professional fine artist and has held multiple exhibitions internationally. Her main subject matter almost always incorporates animals or humans, particularly faces of people of different backgrounds and walks of life different from her own. She loves to create artwork that has significant meaning and that speaks a message to the viewer.

Tamer Elsharouni is also an achieved professional artist, graduated from the faculty of Fine Arts in Cairo, who has art obtained by collectors worldwide and has his artwork displayed internationally. He has held innumerable private exhibitions and international art awards. He also has a passion to create artwork that impacts people and society as a whole. He speaks at conferences and seminars internationally equipping other artists.

Tamer and Cindy now work on projects together. They have put together this book as an endeavor to allow others who don't like to label themselves as artists, to take part in an artistic process. They believe everyone has the potential to be an artist. Anyone can create in a form of expression.

Together, when possible, they finish off each other's work and also enjoy critiquing each other's work. They hope you enjoy the images in this book but even more so the process.

Made in the USA
Lexington, KY
03 December 2017